HOW? WHO? WHAT? WHEN? WHERE? WHY?

Questions kids ask

ABOUT
BIRDS

PUBLISHER	Joseph R. DeVarennes	
PUBLICATION DIRECTOR	Kenneth H. Pearson	
ADVISORS	Roger Aubin	
	Robert Furlonger	
EDITORIAL SUPERVISOR	Jocelyn Smyth	
PRODUCTION MANAGER	Ernest Homewood	
PRODUCTION ASSISTANTS	Martine Gingras	Kathy Kishimoto
	Catherine Gordon	Peter Thomlison
CONTRIBUTORS	Alison Dickie	Nancy Prasad
	Bill Ivy	Lois Rock
	Jacqueline Kendel	Merebeth Switzer
	Anne Langdon	Dave Taylor
	Sheila Macdonald	Alison Tharen
	Susan Marshall	Donna Thomson
	Pamela Martin	Pam Young
	Colin McCance	
SENIOR EDITOR	Robin Rivers	
EDITORS	Brian Cross	Ann Martin
	Anne Louise Mahoney	Mayta Tannenbaum
PUBLICATION ADMINISTRATOR	Anna Good	
ART AND DESIGN	Richard Comely	Ronald Migliore
	George Elliott	Sue Wilkinson
	Greg Elliott	

Canadian Cataloguing in Publication Data

Main entry under title:

Questions kids ask about birds

(Questions kids ask ; 7)
ISBN 0-7172-2546-1

1. Birds—Miscellanea—Juvenile literature.
2. Children's questions and answers.
I. Smyth, Jocelyn.   II. Comely, Richard.   III. Series.

QL676.2.Q47 1988   j598   C89-093160-7

Questions Kids Ask . . . about BIRDS

continued

How many different types of birds are there?

Which kind of bird would you rather be? There are over 8700 types, or species, of birds to choose from.

Perhaps you picture youself soaring high up in the air on enormous wings like an eagle. This bird has sharp claws to grab its prey, a hooked beak and amazing eyesight. There are many birds of prey, including hawks and owls.

Maybe you would rather be a water bird, swimming around lakes or splashing through ponds and marshes. If that's your fancy, you might choose to be a beautiful mallard or an elegant swan or a diving loon.

You might want to be an ostrich. It is the largest bird of all. With its long legs it can run very fast over the dry African plains. The ostrich is one of the flightless birds, like the kiwi and the penguin.

If none of these

birds are to your liking, you could be a perching bird like a robin or a parrot with bright feathers. The variety of size, color and behavior is almost endless. And best of all, birds are found all over the world, from the frozen polar regions to tropical forests. So take your pick.

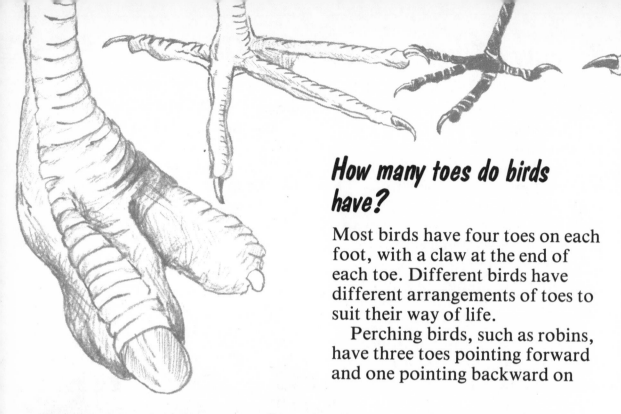

How many toes do birds have?

Most birds have four toes on each foot, with a claw at the end of each toe. Different birds have different arrangements of toes to suit their way of life.

Perching birds, such as robins, have three toes pointing forward and one pointing backward on

Why doesn't a sleeping bird fall from its perch?

When you go to sleep, you lie down. So do most animals. Not birds, however. Most birds sleep standing up! How do they do it?

As a bird settles down to sleep, its specially equipped ankles bend backward and downward. This clamps its toes tightly around the perch. The bird's weight keeps its legs and toes in this position while it is asleep. Its toes can't be unclamped until the bird wakes up and straightens its ankles.

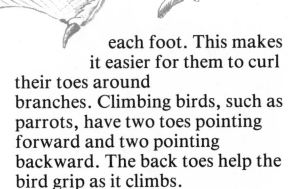

each foot. This makes it easier for them to curl their toes around branches. Climbing birds, such as parrots, have two toes pointing forward and two pointing backward. The back toes help the bird grip as it climbs.

Some birds run instead of flying. It is interesting to note that most of these birds have only three toes on each foot, all of which point forward. The ostrich is a running bird, but it is unique among all the birds in that it has only two toes on each foot.

Why don't penguins get frost-bitten toes?

You would never think of going out in the winter without wearing socks and boots. But penguins, who live mostly in the Antarctic, can walk on ice in bare feet without minding at all.

A penguin's body is perfectly suited for life in a frozen world, and its feet are no exception.

They have many tough little pads on the bottom and these are the only areas that touch the ground. As well, if penguins are standing around, they will always keeps a portion of their feet off the ground by rocking back and forth.

What happened to the dodo?

In 1507, Portuguese sailors discovered the island of Mauritius in the Indian Ocean. They found many animals on the island that they had never seen before. One of these was the dodo.

Dodos had a huge, rounded beak, short legs and a plume-like tail with curly feathers. They weighed as much as 22 kilograms (50 pounds). Their short, stubby wings couldn't lift their weight, so dodos couldn't fly. They laid their eggs and lived on the ground.

Dodos are well-known birds, but no one alive today has ever seen one—or ever will! Dodos have been extinct for about 300 years.

After the sailors, more people traveled to Mauritius. They killed the dodos for food. The animals they brought with them—goats, pigs, rats and dogs—ate and trampled the dodos' eggs, and fewer and fewer young dodos hatched. By the late 1600s the last dodo bird had died.

What does a tailorbird do?

A tailor sews clothes, but a tailorbird sews its own nest.

First it selects a large leaf and folds it in half. Then it sews up the sides. For thread, it uses spider silk, string, wool or the fibers from tough old plant stems. For a needle, the bird uses its bill, pushing the thread

What's so special about the bowerbird?

Where do some birds take their girlfriends on a date? The male bowerbird builds a very special hideaway, or bower, in which to woo a mate. The bower may be as big as a child's playhouse. To build it, the bowerbird collects twigs, vines and moss, and weaves them together with his beak. Next, he takes a twig, dips it in juice from crushed fruit, and paints the bower a bright color. (Very few animals can use tools in this way.) Finally, the bowerbird adds decorations—berries, feathers, exotic flowers. If these decorations fade, he replaces them with fresh ones. When the bower is ready, the bird attracts a mate with songs and dances. But when the honeymoon's over, the birds move to a plain old nest in a tree, just like many other birds!

through one side then pulling the stitch tight from the other. Finally, the tailorbird adds soft grass to make the nest cozy.

You could make a similar sort of home by hanging a sleeping bag from a branch. You don't fancy the idea? I guess you could say it's "for the birds!"

Do all birds sing?

Almost all birds have voices, but they don't all sing. Basically, birds make two types of sounds—calls and songs. Calls are short, have only two or three notes, and are used mainly to give other birds information about food or approaching danger. Songs last longer and have many different notes that follow a pattern.

It is usually the male bird that does most of the singing. He sings to attract a mate and to warn other birds to stay away from his territory. Some birds sing duets with their mates. Other birds sing to keep their flock together while they are flying south for the winter.

While most birds sing, some are only able to make calls. Ducks quack, geese honk, owls hoot, peacocks scream, doves coo, loons laugh, killdeers whistle, and crows, ravens and magpies caw. These birds have voices and can communicate, but they never sing.

DID YOU KNOW . . . the white stork has no voice at all. It makes sounds by clattering its large bill.

Do talking parrots understand what they say?

If you say "Hi!" to a talking parrot, it might say "Hi!" back. But if you then ask it "How are you?" it may not give an appropriate answer. Perhaps it will say "Hi!" again. Or "Who's a pretty bird?" Or even "Goodbye!"

Parrots are mimics—they learn to imitate words and phrases that their owners teach them. They

Do birds have ears?

Think of all the birds you see around you. Do they have ears sticking out from the sides of their heads? No—but that doesn't mean they don't have ears. It's true that they don't have outer ear flaps like you, but they do have a hidden ear hole on each side of their head underneath their feathers.

Many birds have excellent hearing and are quickly aware of the slightest movement. This helps them find food, protect their young and stay out of danger.

DID YOU KNOW . . . some owls hear so well that they can catch a mouse in complete darkness, just by the sound it makes.

don't know what the words mean. It's just by chance that they sometimes say the "right" thing.

But be warned: a parrot may say any of the things it has learned at any time. So if you have one, don't teach it anything that might get you into trouble someday!

11

What makes a flamingo pink?

Does anyone in your neighborhood have a plastic flamingo in the garden? Can you imagine having a real live flamingo? Picture it standing perched on one leg outside your home: a graceful bird with lovely pink feathers. The neighbors would be amazed.

But then what happens? Oh no! Your pet flamingo is turning white! You've been feeding it delicious algae. What's gone wrong?

Flamingos are born gray. They turn pink as they grow up because they eat shrimp that is pink. Shrimp is easy to find in the marshes of the subtropical regions where many flamingos live. But without its shrimp, the poor bird loses its lovely pink color.

DID YOU KNOW . . . zoos have to feed their flamingos a special food that contains the right pink substance to prevent the birds from going white.

It must have been something I ate.

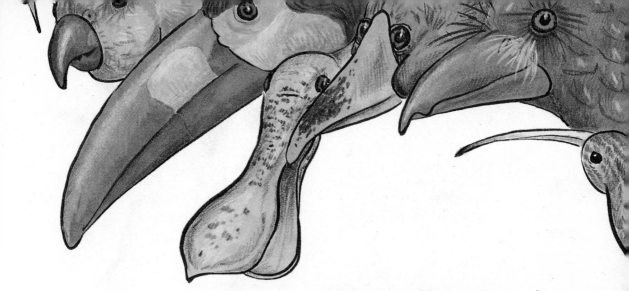

Why do flamingos stand on one leg?

A flamingo's body does not have as many joints as yours does, so its body is not nearly as flexible. Strong muscles enable the bird to keep its body very rigid. Because of this, a flamingo can balance on one leg with very little effort.

Nobody knows for sure why flamingos stand this way. It may be to warm one foot close to their body feathers—or it could be just a way of resting one leg at a time.

Flamingos are not the only birds who like to stand on one leg. Ducks and geese and herons do it too.

Why do different birds have different beaks?

Birds can't hold knives and forks —they have to use their beaks to eat. As a result, their beaks are shaped to help them eat the food that suits them best. For example, ducks have broad bills that help them catch bits of water weed floating in ponds. Eagles have sharp, hooked beaks that they use to tear apart meat. Hummingbirds have long, thin bills they can poke into flowers to reach the nectar within. Finches have short, strong beaks that help them crack seeds.

Because their beaks are just right for eating their favorite foods but are not much use for other foods, birds don't have to eat things they don't like!

13

What animal travels farther than any other animal each year.

The Arctic tern is a world record traveler. Each year in late August, this bird heads south to the shores of Antarctica—a distance of about 17 700 kilometres (11 000 miles)! Months later, it flies back to the Arctic to breed, arriving in mid-June. This is a round trip of about 35 000 kilometres (22 000 miles). To travel as far as an Arctic tern does in ten months, a person would have to run almost three marathons every day!

How do homing pigeons know where to go?

This is a question that still puzzles scientists. Some believe that pigeons use the sun and the stars as well as their sense of smell to help them find their way home from strange places. Others suspect that homing pigeons have some sort of compass in their bodies that responds to the earth's magnetic field. Everyone agrees that pigeons, like all birds, have excellent vision. This helps them recognize familiar landmarks, mountains and vegetation when finding their way home.

Pigeons have been used since ancient times to carry messages. They can fly long distances and still return home. In World War I, a famous pigeon called ''The Mocker'' was given a medal for delivering the message that stopped an enemy advance.

Although homing pigeons are no longer used by the military other people still use them for carrying messages. And some even race the birds. Homing pigeons have been clocked at speeds of 145 kilometres (90 miles) per hour.

DID YOU KNOW . . . at least 36 kinds of birds can find their way home, including the Manx shearwater, storks, swallows and starlings.

15

How did the secretary bird get its name?

Have you ever been busy writing or drawing, and lost your pencil under all the paper you were using? It's easy to do, isn't it? Long ago, secretaries and other people used large, stiff feathers called quills for pens. They put their quills where they couldn't lose them: behind their ears!

If you look at a picture of the secretary bird, you can see that it has tufts of feathers sticking out from the sides and back of its head. These feathers make it look like a secretary from the old days with a quill pen behind the ear. That is how it got its name.

Just in case you were wondering, the secretary bird cannot type or answer the telephone!

Which bird can walk on water?

Although many birds wade in water, only one bird walks *on* water. The Mexican jacana, a small tropical bird, hops from one lily pad to another in its search for tiny water insects to eat. It has long, skinny toes that enable it to spread its weight evenly over each lily pad. This prevents it from sinking. To say the Mexican jacana walks on the water might be exaggerating a little, but it almost does. No wonder its more popular name is the lily trotter!

Why is the nuthatch an unusual bird?

The nuthatch is an unusual bird. Short and stubby, it walks stiffly headfirst *down* trees instead of up them. It is able to do this because it has a much enlarged back toe that gives it secure footing. Anchoring itself upside-down, the nuthatch uses its long, pointed beak to search for insects in the bark of a tree. By going down instead of up, it finds insects missed by other birds.

The nuthatch believes in looking ahead. If it finds more seeds, acorns and other nuts than it needs, it sticks them in the cracks of the bark. When it gets hungry again, it finds one of its hidden treasures and uses its beak to hack away at the nut's shell to break it open. That is how the nuthatch got its name—it was originally called the "nuthack."

DID YOU KNOW . . . the albatross takes off by running over the water while holding its wings outstretched until it lifts off in the breeze.

If you see a cormorant standing on a rock by the shore holding its wings outstretched, it is probably drying its wings. Cormorants spend most of their time diving for fish. If they want to fly to another fishing spot, their wings must be completely dry. Unlike those of most birds, the feathers on a cormorant's wings are not completely waterproof.

Cormorants, also known as sea crows or shags, are related to pelicans. They have long necks and bills and are shaped rather like large black bowling pins. They are such good fishing birds that people sometimes use them to catch fish.

Why do birds take baths?

Sometimes, in hot weather, birds take baths to cool off. And sometimes they may bathe just for fun. But mainly, birds take baths to keep their feathers clean. Birds will bathe just about anywhere—birdbaths, puddles and even overturned garbage can lids. They shower too, hitting wet leaves with their wings to knock dew or raindrops over themselves. After its bath, a bird carefully strokes each feather with its bill until all are neat and smooth. Then it grooms them with oil that comes from a gland near the tip of its tail.

Some birds, such as herons, have a patch of feathers called powder-down. This breaks up into a powder that the bird spreads over its other feathers, like a dry shampoo.

Other birds, such as chickens, grouse and house sparrows, take dust baths. They fluff their feathers and flip dust over their bodies with their wings. Then they shake the dust off and preen their feathers—a very odd way to take a bath!

Can birds fly backward?

Wouldn't it be funny to see a flock of birds flying backward? Unfortunately you never will. Hummingbirds are the only birds that can fly backward—and they do not fly in flocks.

The hummingbird's flight muscles in proportion to the rest of its body are the largest in the animal kingdom. With its special shoulder joint, the hummingbird can beat its wings as many as 80 times per second.

Because of the quickness of its wing beat and its specially shaped wings and shoulder joints, the hummingbird can perform more flying maneuvers than any other bird. It can hover in one place, fly slowly or rapidly forward, up or down, sideways and even backward.

DID YOU KNOW . . . some airports have bird scarers so that birds don't get in the way of the airplanes.

Which bird has the largest wingspan?

People who sail the oceans can sometimes see a huge seabird following them. It flies high above them and never seems to flap its wings. It appears to glide along on outstretched wings for hours.

This bird is the albatross and it has the largest wingspan of any bird. If you measured from the tip of one outstretched wing to the tip of the other, you would find the distance to be over 3.5 metres (almost 12 feet).

Can birds fly as high as airplanes?

Many birds do not fly very high. You can see them flap from one treetop to another, while small aircraft hum far above them.

Some birds, however, fly very high indeed. Birds that are on a long journey often go way up into the sky. The pilot of an airplane was once flying high above the clouds when he saw a flock of whooper swans go by. His airplane and the swans were both about 8200 metres (27 000 feet) in the air—about the same altitude a passenger jet reaches.

So if you're traveling by plane one of these days, try to get a window seat. You never know: you just may look out and see a swan fly past your window!

DID YOU KNOW . . . most birds do not fly above 900 metres (3000 feet).

Which bird lays the largest egg?

It's quite simple. The largest egg is laid by the largest bird in the world—the ostrich. The average egg laid by this flightless bird is about the size of a cantaloupe and weighs 1.5 kilograms (3 pounds). Its thin, white shell is strong enough to support the weight of a burly football player.

Monkeys, snakes and vultures like to eat ostrich eggs—so do many people. One ostrich egg will make an omelette large enough for 12 people.

DID YOU KNOW . . . it takes two hours to hardboil an ostrich egg!

How does a bird get out of its shell?

It may seem very easy for you to break through to the inside of an egg, but it is hard work for a tiny chick to break out of one!

When a chick is nearly ready to hatch, it develops a little bump on the end of its bill called an egg tooth. It uses this egg tooth to chip a hole in the egg shell. If you watch a chick hatch, you may

Where does the cuckoo lay its eggs?

Baby birds are a lot of work for their parents. The eggs must be kept safe and warm for days and days. When the chicks hatch they must be fed until they are able to look after themselves.

Many types of cuckoos have a way to get around all this hard work. The female lays her eggs in other birds' nests. Usually she chooses the nests of smaller birds, and she put only one egg in each. The foster parent keeps the cuckoo egg warm along with her own. Because cuckoo eggs hatch quickly the cuckoo chick is usually the first one out. And it's always hungry. It keeps foster parents busy just feeding it and sometimes the other chicks go hungry.

Boy, am I tired.

hear a faint tapping from inside the egg as the baby bird works with its egg tooth to crack and then make a small hole in the shell. You may even see the tip of the bill poking through the hole. The chick keeps chipping away at the inside of the egg until the hole is wide enough for it to wriggle out.

Once the chick is hatched, the egg tooth falls off or gradually disappears.

Are birds born with feathers?

There are two types of baby birds, and only one is born covered in down feathers. Downy bird babies are the ones you will see most often. These include baby chickens, ducks, geese, ostriches, swans and turkeys. They are able to see from birth, and they are strong enough to leave the nest and run around in the open very early in life.

Most species of birds, however, have babies with hardly any feathers. They cannot see and are very weak, so they stay in the nest and are fed by their parents until they become stronger and grow the feathers they need to fly. As a result, you will rarely see one of these featherless chicks, even though they are the more common of the two types of baby birds.

Why are most birds' belly feathers a lighter color than their back feathers?

The light color of a bird's belly feathers makes it difficult for the bird to be seen from below. Any animal looking up would have a hard time seeing the bird against the sky. This helps to keep the bird hidden and safe from danger.

DID YOU KNOW . . . blue jays are born naked, thus the expression "naked as a jay bird."

But the bird also needs protection from overhead enemies such as birds of prey. Seen from above, the dark back feathers blend in with the ground and the trees, making the bird difficult to spot.

Why are the male birds of some species so brightly colored?

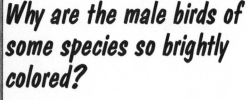

Have you ever noticed how brightly colored a peacock or a male cardinal is? The males of many bird species display brilliant colors—especially compared to the drab females they select as mates.

Scientists have noticed that the male's colors are brightest during the mating season. Is he trying to impress a female with his beauty? Not really. It appears that the brilliant coloring of the male is aimed less at the female of the species than at other males. The vivid color shows that he is in good condition to defend his piece of land. It is a way of advertising his health and strength to other males to keep them away.

While the female is attracted to the male, it is not because of his beauty. A male bird with a territory that will support her babies is what the female looks for. So it is a secure home she wants, not a handsome mate!

Do all birds build nests?

No, not all birds build nests. Some have developed other ways to keep their eggs safe.

Whippoorwills lay their eggs on a bed of leaves on a patch of dry ground. The chicks are born covered in a down of yellowish brown that blends in with the dead leaves around them. This keeps them safe by making them difficult to see.

Nighthawks also avoid the bother of nest building. They lay their eggs on the ground or even on a flat roof. Again, both eggs and chicks are protected by their color. The killdeer lays its eggs anywhere at all—in fields, pastures or even on baseball diamonds. When the eggs hatch, the mother simply leads her chicks away.

Emperor penguins have the strangest habit of all. After the female lays the egg the male carries it around. He holds the egg on his feet, and the heat from his belly keeps it warm until it hatches.

A number of birds use the nests of other birds. House wrens and starlings occupy woodpecker holes, and the house sparrow takes over the nest of the purple martin.

DID YOU KNOW . . . a Carolina wren was once found in the pocket of a coat worn by a scarecrow! Another was found in a clothespin bag that hung on a clothesline.

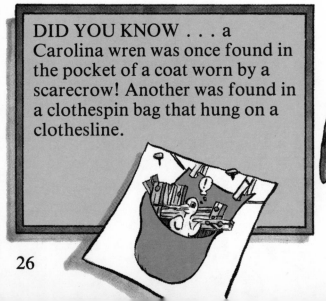

Which bird has the largest nest?

Eagles build the biggest nests, and they build them to last. The largest nest on record was made by a pair of bald eagles in Florida; it was almost 3 metres (10 feet) wide and more than 6 metres (20 feet) deep. It weighed over 3000 kilograms (6600 pounds) and was used for 35 years.

Compare this to the smallest nest in the world—it belongs to the bee hummingbird and is about the size of a thimble.

Which birds build nests underground?

We usually think of birds' nests as being built in trees, but some birds build their nests under the ground!

Bank swallows dig into sandy banks, clinging to rocks or tree roots as they hammer and scrape the dirt out. The finished home has a curved ceiling and is a metre (3 feet) deep.

The kingfisher, shelduck and sand martin dig long tunnels in the ground and deposit their eggs at the end of them. The sand martin and shelduck line their nests with soft feathers, but the kingfisher lines its nest with prickly fish bones. How would you like that for your bed?

DID YOU KNOW . . . marsh birds called grebes build their nests on rafts they make from decaying plants.

27

Why do some birds swallow stones?

Since birds do not have teeth, they swallow their food without chewing it. The food passes into a special pouch inside their bodies called a gizzard. The strong muscles of the gizzard squeeze the food into a soft mush so that the bird's body can digest it.

Birds that eat hard foods often swallow stones or pieces of shell to help the gizzard do its work.

Mmm - stones!

The sharp edges of these hard objects help to cut the food up as the gizzard squeezes it all together.

Do chickens have lips?

Why did the chicken cross the road? Not to buy lipstick!

Chickens do not have lips. Like all birds, a chicken has a hard beak (also called a bill) attached to its jaws. A chicken's beak is short and thick—perfect for pecking hard barnyard seeds.

And it's a good thing chickens don't have lips! If they did, how would a chick peck its way out of its eggshell? How could it preen its feathers to keep clean? How could it peck away enemies?

But then again, a chicken might find lips very useful. It could play a trumpet, blow up balloons, kiss Kiss?! Would you kiss a chicken?

Does a pelican store fish in its bill?

A wonderful bird is the pelican.
Its bill will hold more
than its belly can.

A pelican has an enormous bill which could hold several medium-sized fish at once—but it doesn't. Instead the bird only catches as much as it can swallow at one time.

This large water bird has a long pointed bill with a skin pouch attached to the lower half. It uses the pouch as a scoop to gather fish out of the water. The expandable pouch can hold up to 11 litres (12 quarts) of water, which the pelican forces out of its mouth before swallowing its catch. It feeds mainly on fish and small water creatures called crustaceans.

Pelicans have unique ways of catching their dinner. The smaller brown pelican flies high above the water and then dives when it sees something tasty. The force of the bird hitting the water stuns water creatures for up to 2 metres (6 feet) below the surface. Then it simply scoops up the surprised fish and crustaceans in its bill. The larger white pelican searches for food in groups. The birds swim in a line toward the shore, beating their wings on the surface. This drives fish toward the shallow water where it is easy for the pelicans to catch them. No matter which fishing method is used an adult pelican can devour up to 2 kilograms (4-1/2 pounds) of fish a day.

Are owls wise?

For the ancient Greeks, the owl was a symbol of wisdom. People used to fear and worship it because of its strange calls, its knowing look and its ability to fly without a sound. They thought the owl was a spirit with magic powers.

In fact, scientists seem to think that the owl isn't nearly as intelligent as the blue jay, the raven or even the supposedly silly goose. So how did owls get their reputation for being so wise?

Well, owls certainly *look* wise. Their enormous eyes always seem to be studying things, and the rings of curved feathers around them remind us of the big round glasses professors are often pictured wearing. And if you look wise and people don't know much about you, they are inclined to think you *are* wise. Because most owls are active at night, it is not easy to watch them as they go about their daily routine. We now know more about them than the Greeks did, but many of their ways and habits are still a mystery to us.

DID YOU KNOW . . . owls see better in poor light than you do. But they are *so* farsighted they have trouble seeing their own feet!

Do roosters only crow in the morning?

A rooster, or cock, is a male chicken. Any farmer who has one is greeted each morning at dawn with the familiar "cock-a-doodle-do" wake-up call from the barnyard. The rooster's morning crow lets the hens know that their leader is awake and their territory is safe, so it's time to get up and get on with the day.

The rooster's most important job is to defend his hens and his

DID YOU KNOW . . . the loon, known as the Great Northern Diver, can remain under water for as long as eight minutes!

Why do loons laugh?

Have you ever wondered why people use the word "loony" to describe someone who is a little crazy? If you have ever heard a loon in the wild, you know the strange and haunting calls it makes. One of them sounds like crazy laughter.

But loons aren't crazy despite their strange laugh. It's more likely that the loon is worried. A strange loon may have flown into its territory, or something may be threatening its baby or its mate. Loons are very loyal to their families. Often when you hear one loon laughing you soon hear another one answering.

Other loon calls mean different things. The one that sounds like a yodel is really a love song to a female combined with a warning to other male birds to stay away.

territory. He tells everyone the territory is his by flapping and beating his wings together above his back and crowing as loud as he can. He does this each and every morning if all is well, but he might repeat the ritual several times through the day. If he could talk, he'd be saying: "Stay away, or else!"

Index _____